A Note to Pa

DK READERS is a compelling program for beginning
readers, designed in conjunction with leading literacy
experts, including Dr. Linda Gambrell, Director of
the School of Education at Clemson University.
Dr. Gambrell has served on the Board of Directors of
the International Reading Association and as President
of the National Reading Conference.

Beautiful illustrations and superb full-color
photographs combine with engaging, easy-to-read stories
to offer a fresh approach to each subject in the series.
Each DK READER is guaranteed to capture a child's
interest while developing his or her reading skills,
general knowledge, and love of reading.

The four levels of DK READERS are aimed at
different reading abilities, enabling you to choose
the books that are exactly right for your child:

Level 1 – Beginning to read
Level 2 – Beginning to read alone
Level 3 – Reading alone
Level 4 – Proficient readers

The "normal" age at which a child begins to read
can be anywhere from three to eight years old, so these
levels are intended only a general guideline.

No matter which level you
select, you can be sure that you
are helping your child learn to
read, then read to learn!

LONDON, NEW YORK, MUNICH,
MELBOURNE, AND DELHI

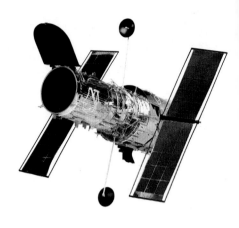

Project Editor Caryn Jenner
Art Editor Jane Horne
Senior Art Editor Clare Shedden
Series Editor Deborah Lock
US Editor Adrienne Betz
Production Shivani Pandey
Picture Researcher Angela Anderson
Jacket Designer Karen Burgess

Space Consultant
Carole Stott

Reading Consultant
Linda Gambrell, Ph.D.

First American Edition, 2001
05 10 9 8 7 6 5 4 3
Published in the United States by DK Publishing, Inc.
375 Hudson Street, New York, New York 10014

Copyright © 2001 Dorling Kindersley Limited

Published in Great Britain by Dorling Kindersley Limited

Library of Congress Cataloging-in-Publication Data
Wallace, Karen.
Rockets and spaceships / by Karen Wallace. – 1st American ed.
p. cm – (Dorling Kindersley readers)
ISBN 0-7894-7360-7 (hardcover) – ISBN 0-7894-7359-3 (pbk.)
1. Space Vehicles–Juvenile literature. [1. Space vehicles.]
I. Title. II. Series.

TL793 .W325 2001
629.47–dc21   00-056974

Color reproduction by Colourscan, Singapore
Printed and bound in China by L Rex Printing Co., Ltd.

The publisher would like to thank the following for their
kind permission to reproduce their images:
Position key: c=center; b=bottom; l=left; r=right; t=top

European Space Agency: 19t, 20t, 29c; N.A.S.A.
24-25 background. **Eurospace Centre, Transinne, Belgium:** 6-7.
London Planetarium: 6. **N.A.S.A.:** front jacket, 4, 5, 8, 9tr, 9b,
10-11, 12-13, 14, 15, 16-17, 18, 26tl, 28-29, 31. **Planet Earth
Pictures:** 22-23, 22b. **Space and Rocket Center,
Alabama:** 24-25 foreground. **Science Photo Library:** 26-27.
N.A.S.A. Kennedy Space Center: front jacket, back jacket.
Paul Weston: illustration 30cl

All other images © Dorling Kindersley.
For further information see: www.dkimages.com

Discover more at

www.dk.com

DK Readers

BEGINNING TO READ 1

Rockets and Spaceships

Written by Karen Wallace

DK Publishing, Inc.

5... 4... 3... 2... 1...
Blast Off!

Rumble... rumble...

ROOAAARRRR!

A rocket takes off
into the sky.
It zooms up and
away from Earth.

rocket

The rocket flies very far,
VERY FAST.

Rumble Rumble ROOAAARRR!

Rockets help us to
explore space.
Astronauts are scientists
who travel in space.

astronaut

They travel in a spaceship
at the top of a rocket.

The rocket takes
the spaceship up to space.
Then the rocket falls away.

Astronauts can see
the Moon and stars
in space.

planet

They can see
planets, too.
Our planet is called Earth.
This is how astronauts see Earth
from space.

Some astronauts have traveled
to the Moon.
They explored the Moon
and did experiments.

They picked up
dust and rocks
for scientists to study
back on Earth.

Sometimes, astronauts
"walk" in space.
Walking in space is not
like walking on Earth.

Astronauts must use a special rope which keeps them
attached to their spaceship.
Otherwise, they would float away!

This is a space shuttle.
It is part rocket, part plane.
Astronauts have used it
for many trips to space.
The plane part of the space shuttle
can be used again and again.
It takes off like a rocket,
then it glides back to Earth
and lands like an airplane.

rocket engine

The space shuttle uses
rocket engines to blast off.
When the rocket engines fall away,
the shuttle plane flies into space.

A space shuttle does
many different jobs.
It can carry satellites
as well as astronauts.

satellite

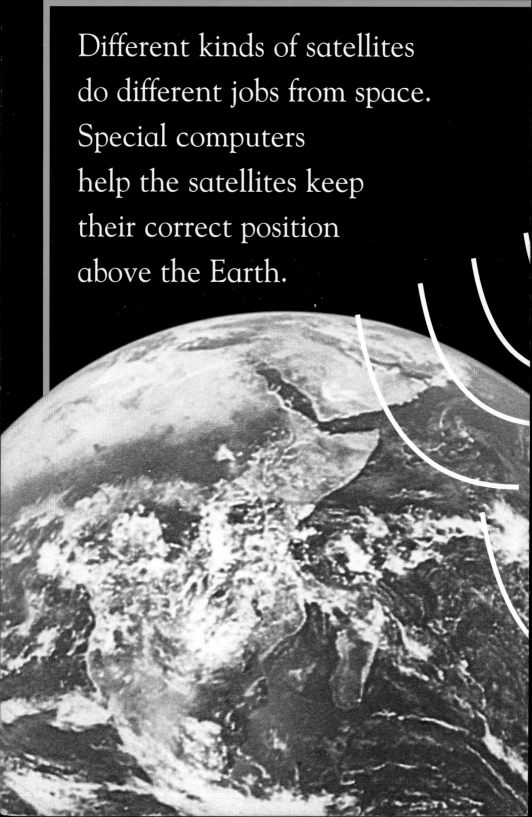

Different kinds of satellites
do different jobs from space.
Special computers
help the satellites keep
their correct position
above the Earth.

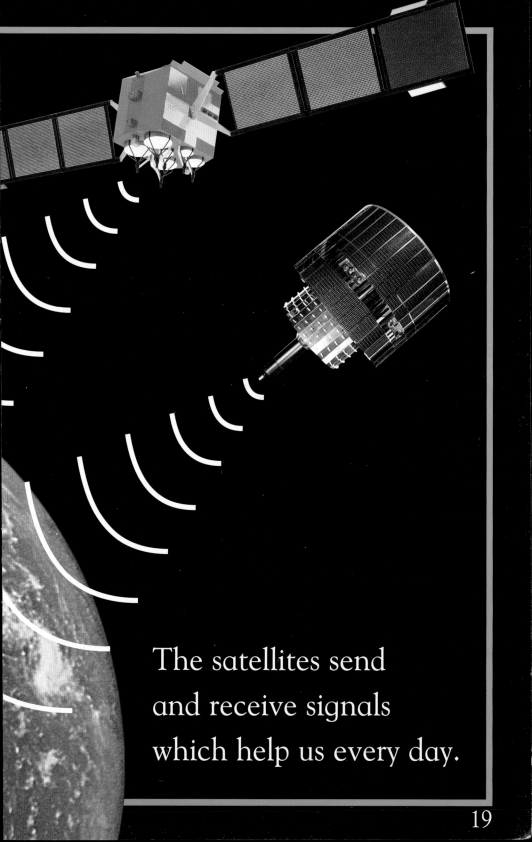

The satellites send
and receive signals
which help us every day.

Some satellites send signals from one part of the world to another.

We use these signals when we watch television or talk on the telephone.

Other satellites
take pictures
of the weather from
high above Earth.

This picture shows
a storm coming!

The Hubble
Space Telescope
is a very
special satellite.

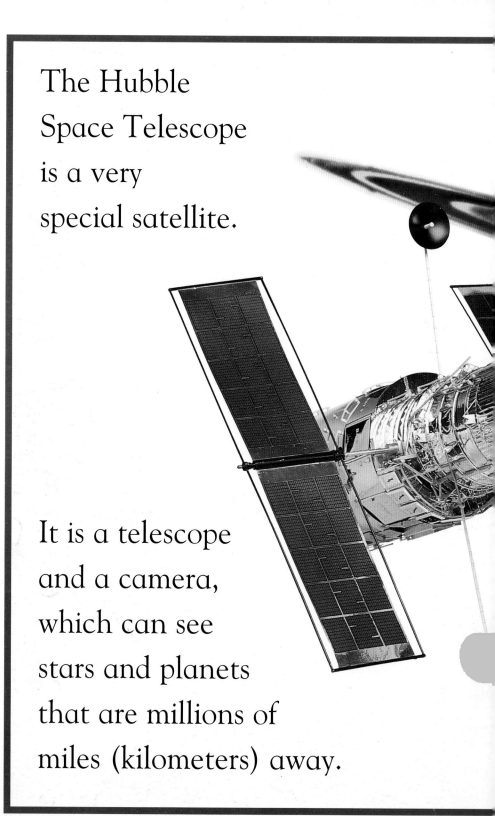

It is a telescope
and a camera,
which can see
stars and planets
that are millions of
miles (kilometers) away.

The planet
in this picture
is called Saturn.

Saturn

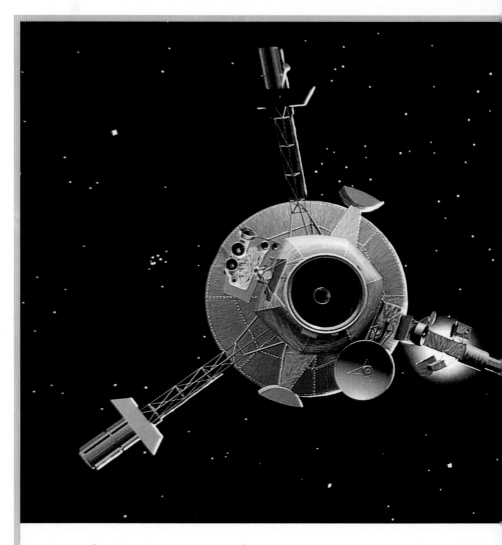

Probes are machines
that explore space
on their own.
They do not carry
astronauts.

probe

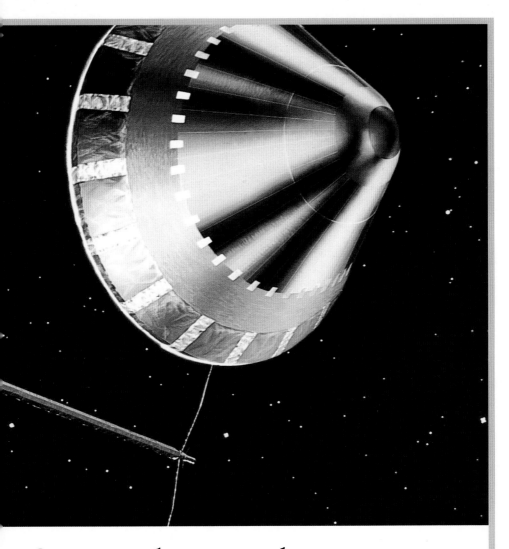

Space probes visit planets
that are very far away.
They take pictures
and send them back
to scientists on Earth.

Mars

A space probe carried
this tiny rover
to a planet called Mars.
The rover explored Mars
and studied the rocks.

Some people think
there might be
life on Mars.
One day, scientists
will know for sure!

Some astronauts
stay in space
for months
and months.

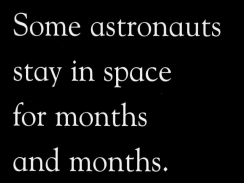

The space station
becomes their home.
They do experiments
and learn about
living in space.

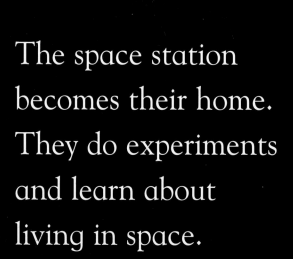

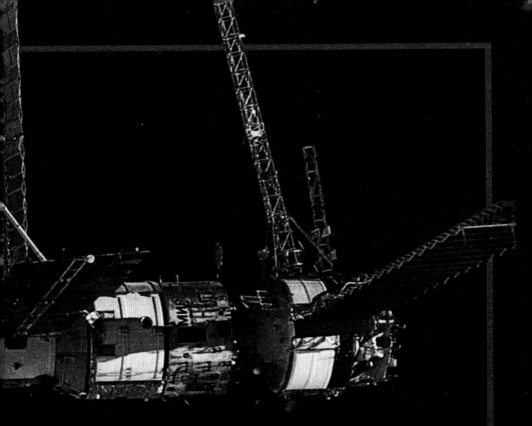

Imagine eating
and sleeping
in a place
where everything floats!

There are still so many secrets
to discover.
Scientists invent new rockets
and spaceships all the time.
There are even plans
to build a space hotel.

Greetings from
space

Who knows?
One day **you** might go
on vacation in space!

Picture word list

 rocket

page 4

 satellite

page 17

 astronaut

page 6

 Saturn

page 23

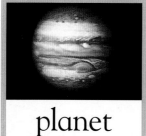 planet

page 9

 probe

page 24

 rocket engine

page 16

 Mars

page 26